ROAR!

April 12, 2015

Empowering Words for Life

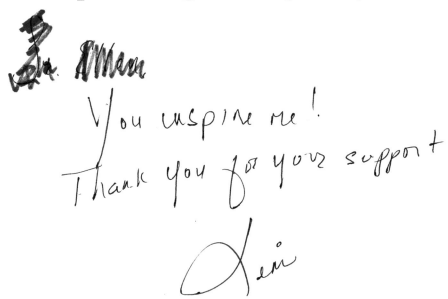

Dr. Amem

You inspire me!
Thank you for your support

Len

LENORE C. UDDYBACK-FORTSON

To order additional copies of this book, contact:
Xlibris
1-888-795-4274
www.Xlibris.com
Orders@Xlibris.com
753141

CONTENTS

POWER IN WORSHIP

POWER IN TRUTH

Dedication

This book is dedicated to
Jesus,
who died so that I might have life more abundantly,
my mom,
who fed my creativity and nourished my love of poetry,
Wes and Noah,
who give me purpose and bring me joy,
and to my elders,
Dr. Edward Mapp, Jessie Birtha and Effie Dawson, who loved on me
when I needed it most,
kept me on a steady diet of their never-ending wisdom, and inspired me
with their walk through life.

To God Be the Glory... Great Things He Has Done!

power in PURPOSE

ROAR!

I am ready to ROAR!
Poised
Moving ahead, light speed
to the echoed rhythm
set by the Lion of Judah

Sound the alarm
Amplify to stir shock waves declaring my place in this world
Mute is no longer an option

I have a voice
Divinely designed to shake naysayers
to the very core of their disbelief
proof of my abilities on full blast

Destiny beckons
I am braced by favor
Roaming my days
Prepared to pounce with precision
To attack opportunity

I claw with vigor
Traps set by the enemy to leave me off-balance, without direction
Or steady footing to ferociously protect my purpose

Life is too short to wish and wonder
Enough of the 'what ifs' and 'maybes'
I'd rather speak up and 'speak life' now
Knowing the true power of my tongue
Acknowledging my true value—priceless

The idea that I am
A destroy-and-discard commodity is a lie
There was/there is meaning in my misery
Messaging meant to bless others
And it's up to me to share
Extend my heart
Use what I've been given
For such a time as this
What time is it?
My time
It's time to ROAR!

Words

Power harnessed
Strength
Breathing life into ideas,
Initiates thought
Sparks action.
Weapons of mass destruction
Or construction,
Depending . . .

The thread of connections
That prompt
Impromptu one-on-ones,
Illuminating likenesses—interwoven attributes,
Undercurrent of a surface existence
All in a matter of seconds.

Words… the backbone of my passion
Brace my intellectual vertebrae;
Fully-loaded ammunition
In the hands of a trigger-happy synapse;

Units in the construct of my story,
The essence of expression,
Releasing verbal shooting stars against the backdrop
Of an infinite expanse of possible life scenarios.

My Pen

My pen is fierce
mighty in battle
bigger
than any fear,
covered by the blood of the Lamb
writing life and light
sharp as the scythe
of God's holy truth
cutting through brambled nonsense.

Pregnant with purpose—
directed,
focused,
the antidote for poisonous tongues
singing false promises,
channeling my heart's desire
to uplift and encourage.

My pen is no joke!
It bears down to birth messages of the Good News,
growing in grace
unobstructed by roadblocks
undistracted by the easy way out.

My pen extends me,
it echoes,
voices dreams,
narrates visions of divine revelation,
Pummels all doubt
with prayer-based responses,
erases clouds of past rejection
and fatigued excuses.
A readied instrument of the Most High,
Who propels my thoughts
with wonder,
as they aspire
to reach His.

It takes me to places
only imagined,
inspiring daily
refreshed determination
to reach,
be stretched,
be emboldened
far beyond my frame of reference.

A vessel of power
in pursuit of peace,
to plant hope,
redirect discussion,
reverse misdirection
rescind misunderstandings and
reiterate intention!

Hmmmmmmmmmm…
My pen is a gift,
a treasure
giving flight to expression,
Offering joy unending
and unquenchable thirst
to keep on writing.

The Messenger

God's messenger spits truth
from love,
Reveals startling images engraved
on a heart of understanding,
Crafts a sequence of words
to breed compassion,
Bears the burden of depicting
an arrested life—barren, arid,
depressed, addicted—
giving rise to voiceless shouts of joy,
muted confessions of gratitude.

But like Jacob to Israel,
Jehovah has changed her name,
and brought her out from under
the thick shroud of deflection.
She flexes wisdom,
masked by beauty
fiercely taking on transparency like a battle,
her true calling,
she waxes poetic.

power in DESTINY

A New Season

Love ushered in a new season;
Unstrapped baggage I carried without reason;
Swept away bitterness that lingered;
Unloaded cares that burdened.

Mercy healed wounds
Lying buried beneath the surface;
And muted memories that caused them to fester.

Grace redeemed time;
Lost in the midst of doubt:
Rescued hope once hijacked by moments of self-pity,
self-destruction;
Whispers of promise
Brought freedom;
Refreshing newness glowing in the light of truth.

ROOTED

you are precious
a creation rooted in love
deep within you lies infinite possibility
awaiting the awakening
of divine promises mirroring world wonders.
your beauty is matchless,
a blossom unfurling,
reflecting the image of our Heavenly Father,
who gifted you with all you need
to realize dreams,
incline hearts,
and bless the lives of others.

Battle Cry

I refuse to wither or lie limp
laden by a label
that does not define me.

This is my fight, and soon,
I'll be armed and ready to fully engage.
Look past this fragile facade,
see the warrior
stained with blood and sweat,
rubbed raw by the grit of determined rage.

Search below and feel
the depth of my strength
unearthed by a flood of my tears,
springing from indelible scars—evidence of hurt
that did not defeat me.

My Favorite New York Native

His wisdom winks at life with assurance—eyes twinkling at the
thought
of a new adventure.
A knowing glance reveals his confidence
in the certainty of uncertainty.

His stature reaches mountain high,
shoulders bearing years of duty
tarrying for change;
observe through the lens
of promise,
hope and possibility.

Deep knowledge carries him
To the visions of his dreams
For himself,
For his children… their children,
For others.

He is at home wherever they take him,
but his heart belongs
to his beloved New York
who stands proud, rich with remembrances,
and birthed his desire
to keep pace with the rhythm of his childhood
and the music of his memories;
to write words that propelled thought,
ushered understanding,
shared his love of cinema,
and made a difference,
carving his place in history.

Mountaintop Moments

Stir your senses,
release your soul,
feel a jubilant freefall
prompted by propelling thrusts of motion.

An eyes-wide-open awakening
sweeping over a panoramic view
through undistorted lenses,
with hopeful filters,
making way for revelations
bursting through,
tearing away at walled emotions,
penetrating ill-perceived obstacles
to clear a path for understanding,
while newness takes over,
feeding possibility,
and opportunity
no longer estranged.

An Angel

An Angel walks among us
And beauty humbly befalls the world;
Shrouded by elegance,
Guarded by wisdom
Directed by the calm voice of reason
Simplicity shines,
Blinding false hope of worldly gain,
Forever giving God the glory.

Strength shields this precious heart,
Relentless faith is reflected,
Resting on the promise
Of purpose manifested,
purified by the blood
of a Savior sacrificed,
suffering in our place,
offering life, light, hope
to empty souls.

An angel walks among us,
Bearing the burden of the lost
Longing to embrace those within reach
To plant a message of redemption
To capture every minute for the Kingdom.

And we,
Who have seen evidence of her grace
Have been touched,
Our lives made brighter,
Understanding deepened,
Pain lessoned,
By the selfless spirit
Of this angel
For whom we are so thankful.

The Little Things

the little things
reflected in the beauty of simplicity
can elevate a weighted spirit
left crushed
beneath the burden of blows
that come so often with life.

daily sky art,
nature's exhibition
on full display for all to see
when the choice is made
to look up
and accept the blessing

musical joy wafting through the air
serenading the listener
with ears
attuned to
welcome its sweet song

the embrace
that finds its way
after a long, exhausting day
offering the kind of pure love
that tickles the heart into sustained submission
and a more relaxed stance.

the briskness of a cool autumn breeze
that alerts us to a new season,
stirring senses,
breathing new life
after the alluring hot trance of summer.

it's all we ignore when
hijacked attentions
and stress-blurred senses,
erase,
or reduce
the value of
the little things.

Solace

I find solace in simplicity.
Taking a step back,
I strip the trappings
of overindulgence,
embracing instead
sweet nothings
that quell manic mental static
and leave me
subdued by quietness.

Freedom finds me
at the heart of this truth
when revelations diagnose
the recklessness of my actions,
and I revel in realness
my need for peace
at the very moment I feel closeted,
alarmingly aimless,
suffocated of voice,
sandwiched between regrets and fears,
muffled by timeless tears,
overwhelmed by the wrongness of it all.

I take shelter in stillness--a motionless moment
caught between pounding heartbeats
coming whenever welcomed,
muting the sound of distraction,
recapturing bleary eyes
by a pattern designed for purpose.

Quiet Grace

Regal, satin stature,
strength burrowed deep
in a foundation of faith
withstanding all worry,
resting on the promise:
life is what it is—equal parts showers and sunshine,
both abundant blessings that
nourish dreams,
summon survival,
stir senses,
feed hope for growth,
reap a harvest of understanding
that silently plows through pain
and undergirds with compassion,
extends a steady hand
and a tender heart
to those desperately in want,
in need and coveting
the comforting stillness
of quiet grace.

power in WORSHIP

God Speaks

God speaks
To the stillness of the heart,
With a voice
That echoes vibrations of peace;
Filling the depth of a soul
When flesh is subdued in submission,
With words that signal cathartic release.

God speaks
Renewal,
Revival,
Hope,
Joy;
In the midst of reflections,
Wondrous revelations.

God speaks
Loudly,
Profoundly,
With deafening clarity;
Distinctively,
Directly,
With purposeful precision;
Softly,
Soothingly,
Sweetly assuring,

Lovingly reminding -- each morning's new mercies

God speaks
God is speaking
Do you hear?
Are you listening?

My Words

The Maker
Gives me words
All—without exception
To use for His glory

A creative brush of His hand
Brings release
For the unique perspective
He embedded in my spirit

Embracing the page with clear devotion
They pour freely
From the depth of me
Longing to reach others
And sweep each place of pain
With His peace

I seek Him with an open heart
So my thoughts
Strive to reach His;
So His words, right and true
Are tightly braided to mine
Without exception

With clear direction
He feeds me hope
That lifts me
Each moment
I secure my gaze on Heaven.
waiting to receive
my words.

Sunrise

God woke me with
a splash of color from His almighty palette,
a breathtaking image for all to behold,
an original work,
an amazing expression of His love and His glory,
a timeless hint of the breadth and depth
of His majesty,
whispering promises
during my own private viewing.

Sunset

God finishes another masterpiece,
blazing fires fill the sky,
golden-red hues initial his canvas,
a custom backdrop
for planes rushing by.

I Want to Be

Lord, I want to be bold,
to bear witness to
newness of life in you,
your love,
faithfulness,
truth;

a truth that sets people free,
releases willing hearts
from a bondage
that cripples,
once perceived unrelenting,
appearing seemingly unhalted;

a truth that delivers helpless hostages
to a paradise on earth,
the abundant life carved by your hand;

a truth that heals deep-cutting wounds
layered beneath the surface
of false appearances;

a truth that lifts forlorn spirits
suffocating under the weight of despair,
and places accessible joy within reach.

Lord, I want to be courageous,
and look beyond selfish fears
that block purpose,
and languish dreams,
contradicting your word.

Lord, I want to be better,
the very image of your intended creation,
a living testimony of your grace,
a reflection of your unending, unconditional love,
the vision of promise,
rooted in belief,
faith,
obedience.

Lord, I desperately want to be,
More
Like
You!

Thank You

Thank you for creating me
on purpose
with purpose
a unique armor of gifts to share,
love to give,
ideas to foster,
dreams to dream
and realize.

Thank you for knowing me
inside and out,
before I even knew myself,
from the vast to the finite intricacies of my being,
numbering the very hairs on my head,
understanding my thoughts and cares
far better than I could ever articulate.

Thank you for loving me
without conditions,
with a reach that escapes limitations,
for seeing beyond each blunder
and careless, selfish act,

for extending an ever-loving arm of forgiveness,
and restoring order
to an all-at-once, out-of-order period in my life.

Thank you for lifting me,
powering me toward destiny,
equipping me
with all I need
to bring your plan to fruition,
and cast my legacy
with intention

Thank you for who you are,
and all that you are to me
at my midnight moment,
in the midst of my fog, uncertainty,
or solemn recognition of painful truth.

You
Are
My
Everything—my hope,
My joy
My light
My rock

Thank you!

Brokenness

In the midst of brokenness,
I learn
perfection is my enemy;
forever mocking me
an aim unattainable
completely out of reach.

My neck no longer feels stiff.
Rigidity—the kind sealed with disobedience—releases its hold.
I am at a place of freedom
and rejoice in my agility,
open to the possibility of change.

Change that once seemed afar
is in view.
A vision of the worn, chipped pieces
taking shape into newness,
feels tangible
and rescues my limp spirit;
revival in its most basic form.

In the midst of brokenness
I wonder at my shift in will,
letting the Potter put me back together again;
my arid soul moistened by tears;
anguish exorcised by a primal cry.

I long to be whole,
right,
real,
ready.
I don't want to miss purpose's next tour;
when it makes a stop all up in and through my life.

In the midst of brokenness,
I let God take over,
relinquish the driver's seat
and just ride,
enjoy the journey,
savor the lessons.
I submit to His control
and soak up His love,
revel in pure contentment
knowing this is all part of His plan.

Fiery Sky

Fiery sky,
bold proclamation
of this brand new day,
explosive streams of color
stampede across God's canvas,
your allure transfixed my mind;
breath held in the balance,
unable to fathom
the gift
of taking in a sight never seen before;
embracing joy,
as pure beauty waved its banner,
marking the territory
of my King of Kings.

Center of His Perfect Will

This fast-paced life isn't really
all it's supposed to be,
ran roughshod,
trampled
leaving behind scattered pieces of me;
true brokenness
at the unfettered hands of ambition.

I shudder,
knowing I buckled
under the power,
pressure of my hustle
dropped to my knees in surrender
undoctored confession
seeking refuge
from a hostile mind takeover.
Directionless,
heart out
in need of a respite--a moment complete
with untangled thoughts
that make way
for peace to prevail.

Weary and worn
desperate to find protection
in the Shadows of the Most High,
who knew all along
this wasn't His plan for me.

I am humbled
as He welcomes me back,
again,
open arms without judgment,
and I resume my place
at the center of His perfect will.

Quiet Conversations

Quiet conversations with my Heavenly Father
soften a hardened edge;
bringing a coolness
that caresses my spirit when worldly angst
obstructs my focus on peace.

Walled in and weighed down,
I succumb to solitude,
take refuge;
my inner sanctuary
that connects with the Comforter.

A momentary hush
subdues the frenetic pace of life,
And I synch with that still, small voice
to receive unending assurances
recalling new mercies,
forgiveness and faithfulness,
an ever-abiding love.

These precious moments
adjust my attitude
and rebuild my stature,
brick by brick,
refortify resistance to strangling
brought on by the strain
of stress and struggle.

Ahhhh… instant sweet relief
riding the tide of timeless promises.

power in TRUTH

Brown Skin

My skin might be brown,
But my mind is alert
And my ears clearly work,
And I know what I heard
When you
Denigrated, disrespected and disregarded me
Momentarily tossing aside the supposed bond we share as
teammates
For the careless use of an ugly word
Anchored by centuries-old pain.

My skin may be brown,
But my heart pumps blood red—just like yours
thick syrup coursing through my veins
Drumming a reminder of the life I've been given
Sometimes punctured by thoughtless acts
hidden under a cloak of privilege.

My skin may be brown,
But my future is high-beam bright
With promise
Directed by my Master's hand
elevated by God's loving plan
Peppered by one-of-a-kind gifts,
Reflected in simple everyday interests

My skin may be brown
But my soul lies layered—buried deep beneath the surface
Of your stereotypical stretch of imagination
You don't even know
All that I am;
All that I will be;
All you see is
my brown skin.

God's People

Where are God's people—those called by His name;
standard bearers for holiness
declaring the rightfulness of righteousness?

Why are cries that could save a nation restrained;
voices instead caught in the trappings of discord,
murmuring dissatisfaction in response to First World concerns,
blurring the lines,
dulling a razor sharp focus on what's truly important, necessary?

Why is humility hidden behind self-centered and selfish pursuits
that supersede open, honest supplication,
with others in mind?

Who seeks the face
of the Most High God,
who waits patiently
to even sense the sense of urgency
our weakened world demands,
its needs constantly drained by our consumption of, obsession
with everyday nonsense?

Is no one laying prostrate,
with open, readied hearts,
waiting to hear from Heaven
on behalf of a land
in desperate need of healing?

Where is the church?

Where
are
God's people?

Just Enough

This morning, in a brief moment of clarity
and brutal honesty,
I had to stop and ask myself,
"Do I really allow You to live at the core of my everything?"

And when I examine my motive in spending time with you,
does it spring from a place of childlike wonder;
a genuine desire to hear from you,
and rest in your presence,
bear my soul when all seems lost,
and await pure restoration,
so clearly aligned with your divine embrace?

Or do I escape to a readily-available excuse of busyness,
revel in rationales
and put in requisite "face time"
when porous sentiment pours from my lips,
reflecting an insincere heart?

Does my commitment lack commitment?

Do I recognize and completely yield to your providence,

yearn to breathe in your sweet quietness

unfailing peace held by the strength of your love?

Do I relish each of your silent calls to my spirit, heed
and fall back in my stillness, recognizing you are God?

Am I straddling, left unsteady
while trying to balance
the false sense of worldly gain
with true wealth
immeasurably found at the heart of spiritual riches?

Am I focused on purpose,
or distracted by vain imaginations
that catch the attention of a side-eye glance,
seeking to move truth from my direct view?

Do I dive head-on and heart-first into your word

in a meaningful way?
Not just because I think I should,

but because I know I am dying of thirst,

in the midst of bone-dry, self-deprivation,

in need of Living Water?

Am I keeping it one hundred percent real--

unmasking the tainted shine others see, my cover

too often revealing a false sense of myself?

Have I submitted to your will,

wrapped in immovable faith,

without reservation,

or am I foolishly trying

to will you to see things my way?

More simply,

am I giving you my all,

or

am I okay with doing,

giving,

being

just enough to get by?

powering my WORDS

Notes

Notes

Notes

Notes

65651503R00050

Made in the USA
Middletown, DE
01 March 2018